Bangaliyana

Advance Praise

'Rajiv Banerjee's illustrations breathe life into the pages of the book, offering a refreshing perspective on Bengali culture. Through minimalist doodles and cartoons, he captures the essence of this vibrant regional culture with remarkable precision. Readers are treated to a unique journey into the heart of Bengali life.'
Sandeep Adhwaryu, chief cartoonist, *The Times of India*

'I am a Tamilian, and I don't consume filter "kaapi". A stereotype that all of us get cast into is what Rajiv Banerjee fights with a "tadka" of humour. As a probashi Bengali who doesn't consume fish, I can imagine what he must have gone through at every family get-together.

My bonds with Rajiv grew stronger than Fevicol when both of us were consumed by the world of brands. If I didn't spot a brand in his inaugural book, I would have been a tad disappointed. A full chapter dedicated to Boroline brings alive the Bengali obsession for the antiseptic cream and made me relive a chapter of our lives as colleagues, when we co-authored an article on regional brands that were intrinsic to our respective cultures.

This is not just a book of cartoons but a whirlwind tour of the Bengali mind. The brand obsessed personas in both of us would probably be tempted to say, Hoodibaba!'
Prasad Sangameshwaran, editor, ETBrandEquity.com,
The Economic Times

'As a probashi Bengali, *Bangaliyana* with its delightful set of stories is imminently relatable. The essence of the Bengali culture is a combination of many things, from food to language to festival, to name a few. Rajiv has captured these nuances very well, both in words and through his cartoons and doodles. I am sure, while reading this book, readers will be taken through a vivid trip down memory lane.'

Deep Dasgupta, former Indian cricket player and now media commentator

'Which came first—the chicken or the egg? For generations, we have been trying to solve the riddle. For Rajiv Banerjee, doodling comes first, ahead of writing. By his own admission, he is a self-taught cartoonist who is still learning the ropes.

The stories on Bengali life and culture, seen through the eyes of a probashi Bengali, complement the doodles and we get *Bangaliyana*. It's not a critique or mockery of the mannerisms and habits of Bengalis but light-hearted observations of the life and times of quintessential Bengalis. The topics vary from daak naam (nickname) to kol baleesh (lap pillow) and Durga Puja to Boroline (typically used for chapped lips, an integral part of a Bengali's life as much as Horlicks and Britannia biscuits).

A fun read for all probashi Bengalis, the book also holds a mirror to those who live in Bengal without malice. Well done, Toton. You guessed it right, that's Rajiv's nickname!'

Tamal Bandyopadhyay, award-winning author and columnist

'The book captures the spirit of a Bengali—from food to language to cinema and culture. Rich in details, Rajiv brings it to life with his sketches. A must-read for all Bengalis to relive Bangaliyana.'

Surojit Gupta, associate editor, *The Times of India*

Bangaliyana

*Doodles, Cartoons and Musings
from a Probashi Bengali*

Rajiv Banerjee

Copyright © 2024 Rajiv Banerjee

Rajiv Banerjee has asserted his rights under the Indian Copyright Act to be identified as the author of this work.

All rights reserved under the copyright conventions. No part of this publication may be reproduced or transmitted in any form or by any means, electronic or mechanical, including photocopying, recording or any information storage or retrieval system, without the prior permission in writing from the publisher.

This book is solely the responsibility of the author(s) and the publisher has had no role in the creation of the content and does not have responsibility for anything defamatory or libellous or objectionable.

BluOne Ink Pvt. Ltd does not have any control over, or responsibility for, any third-party websites referred to in this book. All internet addresses given in this book were correct at the time of going to press. The author and publisher regret any inconvenience caused if addresses have changed or sites have ceased to exist, but can accept no responsibility for any such changes.

ISBN: 978-93-92209-71-0

First published in India 2024
This edition published 2024

BluOne Ink Pvt. Ltd
A-76, 2nd Floor, Sector 136, Noida
Uttar Pradesh 201301
www.bluone.ink
publisher@bluone.ink

Kali, Occam and BluPrint are all trademarks of BluOne Ink Pvt. Ltd.

Contents

Prologue   1

One: Daak Naam   7

Two: Tumi Maach Khao Na!   13

Three: Goto Kaal or Agami Kaal   21

Four: Jamai   25

Five: Kol Baleesh   30

Six: Sunday Breakfast, Lunch and Ghoom   35

Seven: Pujo Pujo Bhaab   40

Eight: Bhog Prasad at Durga Pandal   46

Nine: Pujor Chhuti   60

Ten: Wanderlust   68

Eleven: Aloo Bhaja   75

Twelve: Muchmuche   79

Thirteen: Bhaat	83
Fourteen: Boroline	87
Fifteen: Satyajit Ray	90
Sixteen: Durga Puja Chaanda and Sponsorship	97
Epilogue	102
About the Author	107

To Baba, Ma, Dada, Ishu,
Indrani, Cooper and Chotti

Prologue

I happened to stumble upon the term 'Bangaliyana' on the internet a few years ago. Loosely put, it is about Bengali culture, food, festivals, music, debates and discussions (adda), anything and everything that makes a quintessential Bengali.

I am a probashi Bengali—a term for Bengalis born outside of West Bengal. Being born and raised in Mumbai, the city rules my senses. I swear by Sachin Tendulkar and not Sourav Ganguly, although I will admit Dada infused the much-needed steel in the team's spine during his tenure, both as a player and as captain of the Indian cricket team. Vada pav still commands my palate, although during Durga Puja (a festival celebrated by Bengalis) in Mumbai, it is egg roll and Mughlai paratha with mutton kosha that I, like my fellow Bengali brethren, plunge into. Come to think of it, I have always observed a sea of humanity (read Bengalis) at the food stalls rather than Mother Goddess' idol. Well, to be fair, we Bongs (short for Bengalis) always first pay obeisance to Ma Durga before we head to the food stalls to satiate our hunger pangs.

Cartooning or doodling was always a part of my growing up years. At school, there was not a single notebook left without a doodle or two on every page. Sometimes, it was just faces, sometimes random square lines. I was fascinated by images of fighter planes, helicopters and tanks, so they figured in my sketches most often. Frankly, I was never a meritorious student, and the hour-long classes seemed an eternity; so, sketching was my escape from the drudgery of everyday school. In fact, I slept through my school life. So much so that at the only school reunion that I attended, the teachers struggled to recollect if I was ever part of their class. I was saved from further embarrassment by a bunch of popular and known students from my time who gathered around the teachers. Their befuddled gaze quickly moved away from me, and I fortunately did not have to bear the ignominy of 'no recollection of this boy from the class of 1990'. This situation was best analysed by a school friend of mine, who also faced a similar situation, during the reunion. 'You see. We were both middle benchers. Teachers only remember the front benchers, who were studious and meritorious, or back benchers, who were noisy, mischievous and forever getting into trouble. So, nobody remembers us.' This was his philosophical rumination over Old Monk rum. I could not disagree, and I went bottoms-up on both Old Monk and my slightly hurt pride.

I grew up in the era of *Tinkle* and *Indrajaal* comics. Buying comics, exchanging them with friends and going to the neighbourhood library for a fresh supply was the only way to satiate my appetite for comics. However, it was 'Detective Moochwala', a character by the renowned cartoonist Mr Ajit Ninan in a children's magazine called *Target*, that I would scan with a fine eye. I was simply bowled over by the sketches—the expressions, postures and imageries—soaking in everything with utmost fascination. Those images have remained. Those drawings did lay the foundation of my love for cartooning.

I have had the good fortune of meeting Mr Ninan, and the time spent with him absorbing every word he said remains etched in my memory. 'Take leave for two days and come to Delhi. Stay with me. We will only talk about cartooning,' Mr Ninan had offered. Alas! My trip to Delhi never materialized, and it is the one regret I will carry in my heart for the rest of my life.

From comics, as I graduated to reading a newspaper, the first port of call was always the pocket cartoon. The first newspaper I remember at our home was the *Daily*, which carried a pocket cartoon by the cartoonist Mario Miranda. I remember cutting the cartoon strips and archiving them regularly; at one point of time, I had gathered a respectable collection. Mr Miranda had a distinct style of capturing the human face, and the pocket cartoon gave us memorable characters such as Miss Fonseca, Godbole and Bundaldass to name a few.

From the *Daily* newspaper our family graduated to the *Times of India*, which was when I was introduced to the pocket cartoon 'You Said It' by the great R.K. Laxman, whose 'Common Man' regaled readers for decades. For me, the page-one news and headlines did not hold the same allure as the 'Common Man' pocket cartoons, which I would religiously see to absorb the fluency with which Mr Laxman would bring everyday scenarios to life in black and white.

After completing my graduation, the financially precarious state of affairs at home necessitated taking up a job. Two decades have passed and this treadmill called 'career' continues to move at hyper speed with no brakes. It was in one of those moments when mental and physical fatigue overtook me that I reached out for a black pen and a blank sheet of paper and started to doodle. This was about 8 years ago and akin to riding a bicycle after a long time, where you are rusty at the start but then soon find your balance, doodling and cartooning came back to me slowly but surely. I do not profess to be a professional doodle artist or a cartoonist. I prefer to be known as a self-taught cartoonist who is still learning the ropes. That way, I hope to keep the learning curve alive.

Over the years, I have sketched on various themes but the concept of Bangaliyana has provided me with a rich vein of ideas to doodle. My sketches have emanated from general observations and, in some cases, first-hand experiences in a Bengali household. For example, when it comes to talking in Bangla, Hindi words and phrases invariably flow into my vocabulary as I have always struggled to find the right words in Bangla. I am sure it is the case with many of us who are born outside their native states.

Beginning with *pujo aashchhe* (Durga Puja is nearing) to *pujo pujo bhaab* (Durga Puja is in the air), which every Bengali, be it probashi or resident, will have on their mind as soon as the monsoon recedes, to a light-hearted observation on a Bengali's penchant for food—be it maach (fish), aloo bhaja (deep fried potatoes) or aloo sheddo (mashed potatoes).

So far, the Bangaliyana journey through doodles has covered many destinations, be it the community's general behaviour, food habits, movies, language or even Bengalis' vacation trips. For example, the daak naam (nicknames), mashimas' (mother's sisters') and pishimas' (father's sisters') determination to feed you till your stomach bursts, the look of abomination on the faces of relatives when they hear that you do not eat fish—'*O Ma! Shei ki. Maach khao na*' (You do not eat fish!)—have been captured in this book both in doodles and words.

Bengali movies is another space in this journey that I have attempted to capture through my sketches. Over time, I have become an ardent fan of the well-known author and movie director Mr Satyajit Ray and his body of work, be it his books or movies.

My doodles on Bengalis are not a critique or mockery of the mannerisms and habits of Bengalis but a series of light-hearted personal observations and views expressed through drawings.

This book contains some of my doodles, drawn over the past few years, on Bangaliyana. The journey continues.

ONE

Daak Naam

The relationship between Bengalis and their daak naam (nicknames) is a unique one. For example, an elderly gentleman can be known by his daak naam Khokha (child) in his para (neighbourhood) whilst an eight-year-old girl can be nicknamed Buri (old woman).

The question '*Tomar daak naam ki?*' (What is your nickname?) to a person, well beyond his thirties, at a social event, involving both friends and relatives, evokes trepidation, humour and mirth. To non-Bengalis, hearing your daak naam for the first time generates curiosity about its meaning or a proclamation of its cuteness, leading to frequent leg-pulling.

My daak naam is Toton. Why? I do not have the faintest idea! What does it mean? No clue. Come

A dadu (grandfather) with 'Khoka' (small child) as a daak naam (nickname) and a small girl with 'Buri' (old lady) as a daak naam

to think of it, I never really bothered to ask my parents about it. As a probashi Bengali, my daak naam became my name in the locality I grew up in. It stuck like industrial glue, so much so that any outsider visiting my locality asking for me by my formal name would have the residents befuddled! 'Who is he/she talking about?' They would be left

Bengali daak naam

scratching their heads. After a few more clues about the house address and other minor details, the penny would drop. 'Oh, you mean Toton? He stays right over there.' One of them would even volunteer to take the visitor to my doorstep and holler my daak naam from downstairs, waiting for me or someone

Tomar daak naam ki? (What's your nickname?)

from my family to pop their heads out of the balcony and acknowledge.

For Bengali residents of my locality, my daak naam was Toton, but this was a cosmopolitan society of various communities. The use of the alphabet 'O' while pronouncing the daak naam therefore was a challenge for non-Bengalis. So over time, it became Totan, which is easy on the tongue. And my friends ensured my daak naam acquired a variety of short forms. So, Toton became Totan, which then took on several variations like Toti, Tots and a highly creative Two-Ten. My daak naam and its variations became my personal brand identity in my locality.

The use of daak naam over time has become rare. Today, only my close childhood friends call me by my daak naam. Of course, my close relatives from Kolkata still know me by it, and likewise, I only know my cousins by their daak naams. I do not even know their formal names, and I am sure, they too will struggle to put a face to my formal name even today.

Sometimes, when my childhood friends call me by my formal name, it feels as if there is distance that has crept into the relationship. Using choicest abuses, I reprimand them for not calling me by my daak naam. These relationships are precious, and I feel that our nick names are the the bridges that connect us.

Decades have passed, but the memories associated with my daak naam remain. To the world, I am known by my name. But to the world that is close to my heart, my daak naam still rules. The one voice the heart yearns to hear today is my ma (mother) calling me by my daak naam. It still echoes, only inside me.

To me, this tradition of a nickname is reminiscent of a time gone by, a world within the larger world, of evenings, when the daak naam called out by Ma from home was acknowledged loud and clear by me, even from a distance. It was a signal to wrap up and come home, as dusk was falling.

The legacy of daak naam continues as our daughter has several daak naams.

I am sure that the daak naam of any individual, irrespective of communities, is a sea of memories.

So, *tomar daak naam ki?*

TWO

Tumi Maach Khao Na?

This chapter is dedicated to me and a few other Bengali brethren. Maacher jhol and bhaat (fish curry and rice) is synonymous with Bengalis but imagine the horror on the faces when I announce, '*Ami maach khai na*' (I do not eat fish). The stunned looks, the silence and finally the clucks of dismay as people around me finally muster up words to respond. I think even the maach (fish) in the jhol (curry) pops up wide-eyed and stares at me with utter disbelief.

Many times, my announcement and the disbelieving looks are followed by one last determined effort to get me to consume fish. '*O Ma! Maach khaye na? eie ki Bangali, ektu o khao na? Ektuo na?*' (What! You don't eat fish? Not even a bit?); it

Ami maach khai na! (I don't eat fish)

goes on for some time, till the folks resign themselves to the fact that I indeed do not consume fish.

Okay, so I am a Bengali and I do not eat fish. The truth is, I never really developed a taste for fish right from my childhood. As a child, I could not dare to be vociferous about my dislike for fish with my parents, but as I entered my teens, I made it amply clear to my folks and people around me that I do not

The Richter 9 shock wave in a Bengali household when you announce 'ami maach khai na' (I don't eat fish)

like fish; the only marine food I occasionally eat is prawn.

Even today, in social gatherings, if the conversation veers towards food, my statement 'I do not eat fish' evokes much amusement and puzzled looks. 'A Bong who does not eat fish? How is that possible? You are a fraud Bengali,' is a rhetorical remark one often gets.

Since I never developed a liking for maach, I never bothered to distinguish between an ilish (herring) and a pabda (butter catfish) or a rohu (Indian carp). They all look the same to me. And a few times, my family made the mistake of sending me to the fish market, I felt like a fish out of water. Once I mustered enough courage to ask an uncle standing next to me, '*Kaku, eita ki ilish maach?*' (Uncle, is this hilsa?). His piercing eyes and revolting looks said, 'The temerity to ask me such a question!' With a croaking voice akin to a rohu fish bone stuck in his throat, he pointed towards a bunch of ilish stacked up.

In Mumbai, Bengalis throng the local maacher bazaar (fish market) during the weekend for their weekly supply of tatka (fresh) maach. Today, I like visiting the fish market just to listen to the conversations and observe the mannerisms of the people, all necessary ingredients for my doodles. The local fishmongers do not pay any attention to me, for they seem to know that I do not know my fish. Their prized clients are the kakimas, pishimas, kakus and dadus (aunties, uncles and grandfathers). Most fishmongers have, over the years, picked up a smattering of Bengali phrases to add to their sales pitch, '*Aasun, kakima, ilish nao, khub bhalo*' (Welcome, aunty, there are some good hilsa for sale). With the advent of technology, the fishmonger today sends a WhatsApp message with the day's catch, pictures and price to his loyal clientele. Orders are given and the fish is home delivered. However, most Bengalis like to see, touch and feel the fish before buying it, so technology still has not eaten into the footfalls witnessed at the neighbourhood fish market during weekends.

The kakimas, mashimas and kakus are formidable opponents in a negotiation slugfest with fish sellers. '*Isko tol o.*' Now, it could mean 'pick it up for me to see' or 'weigh it'. But the fishmonger is a seasoned campaigner. He knows exactly what kakima is saying. Lifting the fish, he pulls the gills out for her to see. '*Ek dum tatka hain*' (It is absolutely fresh). Dekhi (let me see), and kakima will personally do a quick post-mortem to validate what the seller is saying. Satisfied, the bout then moves to the price. '*Satsho taka! Ki dakaati hocche!*' (This is daylight robbery). After some intense haggling, both parties arrive at what is called in the art of negotiation a ZOPA (zone of possible agreement). The deal is done. Sometimes, two potential customers, a kakima and a mashima, join forces to negotiate the best price for a fish. Both do not want the whole fish. One prefers the *peti* (the stomach part of the fish), the other the *lej* (the tail), with the head thrown in.

Scenes from a fish market during the weekend

Once the price is negotiated, comes the most intense part, the cleaning and chopping of the fish. Here, the eyes of the seasoned kakimas and kakus will put even the cutting-edge Hawkeye, a technology used in cricket and other sports, nowadays to adjudicate and track the trajectory

A quick adda session at the fish market

of the ball, to shame. Their sheer focus, when the fishmonger starts chopping the fish, is amazing. If the sharp gaze could cut and chop, then the kakimas and kakus in a maacher bazaar would emerge as winners. '*Medium piece karna. Bada piece chai na*' (Cut it into medium pieces; I do not want big pieces), '*Aiyee! Mundi ko two piece mein karo*' (Hey, cut the head into two pieces).

As the fishmonger wraps up the cleaning and chopping, Bengalis do what they do best—a bit of adda (gossip or conversation) over a cup of chaa (tea). There is always a tea seller frequenting the market, particularly during the weekends. He is assured of brisk sales.

Even after so many years, I still get the question at the dining table, *'Maach khabe?'* (Will you eat fish?) or *'Ektu maacher jhol khao'* (Have some fish curry). I say no. As I busy myself with eating what is on my plate, I pick up murmurs and discussions about a Bengali who does not eat fish. Well, it does get *'too maach'* sometimes, but now I just grin and bear it.

THREE

Goto Kaal or Agami Kaal?

Many years ago, I travelled to Kolkata to attend a wedding in my extended family. For ease, I am calling the groom my cousin, else he is my mastoto dada (my mother's sister's eldest son). I was initially apprehensive about being able to converse fluently in Bengali in Kolkata. A few days passed and I patted my shoulder, believing that my Bangla (Bengali) has passed with flying colors. 'I thought you are a north Indian, going by your Bangla,' remarked one bhadralok (gentleman) who I met at the wedding reception. It was like a toe-crushing yorker, to use a cricketing analogy, where the ball not only hits the batsman's big toe but also sends the wicket stumps cartwheeling in all directions. I felt like one such batsman painfully hobbling back to the pavilion.

The goto kaal and agami kaal conundrum

The Bengali gentleman's words were like a pin that pricks a balloon, initially sending it flying upwards and then eventually dropping to the ground deflated. The confidence I harboured on my superb command over my mother tongue now lay in tatters.

As a probashi Bengali born and raised in Mumbai, I have had my share of palpitations and nervousness tingling through my body whilst conversing with Bengalis. It is easy going with a fellow *probashi* Bengali, but I tread with caution while talking to Bengalis from West Bengal.

My Bangla is laced with Hindi words that often substitute the actual Bengali words. The mind processes sentences in Hindi, and the Bengali that comes out is almost a literal translation of the Hindi lines. One example is the use of *goto kaal* (yesterday) and *agami kaal* (tomorrow). My mind is all knotted up trying to decipher whether it means the previous day or the next day. The confusion continues till date despite innumerable efforts by my family to explain the difference. It seems like my brain simply cannot process something as simple as this. I am used to the Hindi word *kal*, which can be yesterday or tomorrow depending on the context. The term in Bangla for 'getting angry' is *raag hochhe*, but I say *raag aashchhe*, the literal translation of which is 'anger coming'. Often, I am corrected for incorrect usage, but they never register. Incidentally, I have never used the term *durdanto*, a term used by Bengalis when they see, hear or read something breathtaking. I visualize the word as a long-range bomber aircraft carry a massive payload. And durdanto happens when the bomber disgorges its payload over the target. If in the midst of Bengalis I have to use a word to express my amazement, I stick to the colloquial Hindi word *sahii*!

As a probashi Bengali, it is natural for your Bengali to acquire the tone and tenor of the region where you were born and spent your life in. I am sure probashi Bengalis from Delhi will have a Delhi flavour in their Bangla. Ditto for Bengalis from UP, Bihar or even South India. Pronunciations also acquire local flavours. For example, I have been corrected many times by my family when I use the words 'dupur' (afternoon) or 'keno' (why). My dupur becomes 'duphur', like the Hindi word 'dopahar'. I pronounce 'keno' with an 'a' as 'kano'. For my family, it continues to be an exasperating exercise to correct my faulty Bengali pronunciation. However, now they just laugh and no longer waste their breath to correct me.

This is the story of my ongoing tryst with Bangla as a probashi Bengali. It is like a minefield that I still walk into. Sometimes I escape unscathed, but sometimes it just blows up in my face. This is not a critique of the Bengali language but rather a joke on me. My family laughs, and I do too. You can laugh as well. Laughing is good.

FOUR

Bengali Jamai

Once I received a WhatsApp photograph of a Bengali *jamai* (son-in-law) posing with a plate full of food and an impressive number of bowls overflowing with even more food. The plate and the bowls, neatly arranged in a circle, resembled Eden Gardens (the famous cricket stadium in Kolkata) with a capacity crowd. This picture was doing the rounds during Jamai Shoshti, a day dedicated to sons-in-law, marked by a grand feast for the jamai. A full course meal is an understatement as one starts losing count of the number of dishes that emerge, thick and fast, from the kitchen. Looking at the spread, one would assume that the jamai would have fasted in preparation for the feast. That is not the case. Jamai Shoshti or not, jamais are

All eyes on the jamai (son-in-law)

usually treated like gods by their in-laws and fed sumptuous food every time they visit.

Indeed, a jamai in a Bengali household is the cynosure of all eyes during Jamai Shoshti. Apart from the occasion being a veritable gastronomical journey, I have noticed all pairs of eyes following every move the jamai makes at the table. It is usually the womenfolk of the house, who surround the jamai. Men of the house simply disappear. It is the sashuri (mother-in-law), mashi-sashuri (aunt-in-law) and countless other womenfolk who ensure no one comes between them and the jamai. Matriarchy simply rules here. The close-body protection skills

A Bengali jamai being loaded with love, affection and, of course, food!

of the womenfolk near their jamai will put even the highly trained Special Protection Group (SPG) guarding the honourable prime minister to shame. One hopes that the wife is around to intervene if the need arises, but alas, she too has abandoned you, leaving you at the mercy of the womenfolk-in-law!

The first sight of the spread looks inviting, but *aasho baba, bosho* (come, dear, please sit) is the start of a marathon. There is a beatific smile on everyone's face, which makes you nervous, causing you to sweat.

Baba, gorom lagche? (Son, are you feeling hot?). Of course, with all the radar-like eyes locked on you, you are bound to feel the heat. But you give a faint smile, mumble something incomprehensible and go back to eating.

There is pin drop silence as everyone watches the jamai eat. It is like match-point silence, as the audience watches the action with bated breath. Suddenly, the reverie is broken by a shriek from the audience around you. '*O Ma! Eie ki? Sob bhaat dal diye shesh korcho je. Aaro khabar aache toh*' (What's this? You are polishing off the rice with just the lentils! There is more to come).

Muri ghonto ta kemon hoyeche? (How is the dish made with fish head?) *Chingri maach aar ektu debo?* (Care for more prawn?) *Aarey mangsho khabe toh* (There's a mutton dish next). Questions are for effect—merely rhetorical. There cannot be no for an answer. You can make feeble protests, but these are brushed away as another large tablespoon of food lands on your plate.

A jamai passes with flying colours when not even a single morsel remains on his plate and the plate is spotless. The eyes around you will indicate if you have passed or flunked the food test. Beaming eyes mean *jamai bhalo khae* (son-in-law ate well); droopy, downcast eyes mean *jamai ekdom khete pare na* (son-in-law cannot eat).

And if the jamai, after the feast, can polish off a few rosogollas (a Bengali sweet) and wash it down with mishti doi (sweetened yogurt), he becomes the apple of everyone's eye.

For sons-in-law who like a good meal, the in-laws always compliment that he eats well. For me, it has usually been 'he cannot eat'. The reason being I do not eat fish, and over the years, my consumption of non-vegetarian food, like chicken and mutton, has reduced considerably. Ditto for sweets. Jamai Shoshti largely is about feeding the jamai with the choicest non-vegetarian fare; with me, it is usually a tame affair. Disappointment looms large on the faces as I dig into lentils and vegetables on my plate with gusto. So, all the jamais who, like me, fall in the *ekdom khete pare na* (poor eater) category, please raise their hands!

FIVE

Kol Baleesh

We Bengalis may be divided into probashi versus native, Bangal[1] versus Ghoti,[2] Mohun Bagan versus East Bengal,[3] etc., but we stand united when it comes to one quintessential possession seen in every Bengali household—the *kol baleesh* (bolster). If pujo, khichuri and omlette during brishti (monsoon) are at the top of the list of favourites, kol baleesh holds its own in that list, almost vying for the top spot in the list of things dear to a Bengali.

The kol baleesh is a family heirloom passed on from generation to generation. A kol baleesh that

---

1 Bengalis who migrated from East Pakistan (now Bangladesh) in 1947 to West Bengal and other parts of India.
2 West Bengalis.
3 Rival football clubs based in Kolkata; While Ghotis support Mohun Bagan AC, Bangals root for East Bengal Club).

Anatomy of a kol baleesh

entered the house when the didun (grandmother) got married is inherited by the son or daughter and so forth. If the family moves cities, the kol baleesh travels too. It usually has a long life, and only when it is in tatters with its cotton stuffing falling out copiously that the family decides to replace it with a new one.

The kol baleesh has high sentimental value for Bengali families. Much like the renowned cartoonist

Bengalis' love for kol baleesh

R.K. Laxman's 'Common Man', who silently watched the meanderings of worldly life, I feel a kol baleesh is the 'common man' of a Bengali household. Over generations, it has witnessed the ups and downs in a Bengali household. Happiness, sorrow, celebrations, grief—it has seen all. The cotton stuffing in the bolster has absorbed tears of happiness and sadness; it has been privy to many conversations—from loud banter to gossip to hushed conspiracy stories. In pillow fights, the person with a bolster always has an edge over an opponent who wields a regular pillow.

From time spent contemplating and ruminating on issues that weigh heavy on the mind whilst resting one's head on the kol baleesh to the happiness of talking to your beloved lying on the bed with the bolster or tears streaming down the cheek onto the kol baleesh as one nurses a heart break—the kol baleesh is a repository of memories. It is an inanimate object, but if the bolster could speak, read and write, it could easily take the role of a chronicler of a Bengali household.

As I entered my teens, I developed an interest in reading on defence and strategy, which continues till date. Back then there was a comic book called *Commandoes*, with stories from the Second World War. It used to be a riveting read, with tanks, war planes and an entire paraphernalia and exploits of special forces working behind enemy lines. These stories fired up my imagination, and I enacted scenes from the battlefield with my kol baleesh as the centre piece! Sometimes, it was an air force base, with paper planes taking off to strafe enemy positions. Mostly, household items such as match boxes, small utensils, pens and pencil boxes doubled up as battle tanks, an army base or a fuel depot. Sometimes, the bolster became a trench behind which, lying prostrate, a sniper, which was almost always me, would take out enemy soldiers. And after some hectic battlefield fighting, the kol baleesh would again become a pillow for a well-deserved rest for a 'battle-weary soldier'.

There is one scenario where the kol baleesh becomes indispensable—*ghoom* (sleep) or sometimes *lyaad khawa* (lazing around). So, imagine a monsoon afternoon at home, where the pitter-patter of the rains activates a primal Bengali urge to have kichuri (a mix of lentils and rice) with an omelette or a maach bhaja (fried fish) or aloo/begun bhaja (deep fried potato or aubergine) for lunch. After the meal, the mind and body become soporific, and one is automatically pulled towards the bed and the kol baleesh.

So, the next time you see the kol baleesh in your house, do give it a reverential glance. For it has been silently providing succour, both mental and physical, to you and your family for generations. Salute!

SIX

Sunday Breakfast, Lunch and Ghoom

Lunch on a Sunday in a probashi Bengali household is an elaborate affair. Typically, nuclear Bengali families, say in Mumbai, usually run through weekdays with a meagre fare, but over the weekend, especially on Sundays, the meal must be elaborate.

It starts with breakfast with a plate of luchi torkari (deep fried wheat flatbread with a potato curry). Sometimes, the torkari also has kumro (pumpkin), mutter (peas) and aloo (potato). After polishing off a dozen luchis with the torkari, everyone is at a heightened state of alertness, to know what is being cooked for lunch. An early morning dash to the market ensures that there is ample supply of

Luchi (puffed round bread fried in oil) with torkari (a potato-based dish) for breakfast and a happy Bengali household

chicken, fish and the necessary green vegetables for a sumptuous lunch.

Lunch begins with a dish that is quintessentially Bengali—shukto (a mishmash of vegetables usually in a gravy) or korola sheddo (boiled bitter gourd) with a dash of shorshe tel (mustard oil) and bhaat (rice). These are the appetizers that set the tone. Or you can call them cleansers. I believe starting a meal with shukto is an acquired taste. As a child, I was elated when I could skip eating anything bitter

Sunday Breakfast, Lunch and Ghoom 37

A full course Bengali meal on a Sunday

like boiled bitter gourd. Today, it is an essential for me. In a Bengali Sunday spread, there is an array of appetizers to choose from apart from bitter gourd; there is boiled pumpkin, beans or even potatoes to be had with mustard oil or ghee (clarified butter).

After the appetizer, it is time for bhaat to be accompanied by dal (lentils), nirameesh torkari (a vegetable dish) and bhaja (fritters). Bhaja, in Bengali families, sits high in the revered list of food items consumed by a household. It deserves a separate chapter, and rightly so. There is a variety of bhaja, from aloo (potato) to begun (brinjal) to

A satiated Bengali, post lunch, catching up on a siesta

potol (pointed gourd). Usually for lunch, it is either aloo or begun bhaja. If it does not figure in the fare, there is open dissent at the table—'*Bhaja nei!*' goes the lament, reverberating from chair to chair, plate to plate. Somehow, the second course of lunch is incomplete without a mouthful of bhaja. Also, it is important to note that bhaat is the common thread in all the courses.

The third course begins with mangshor jhol (chicken or mutton curry) or maacher jhol (fish curry). It is incomplete without a commentary on the taste and texture of the purchase, be it maach or maangsho. Whilst digging into the fish or the meat, there will be a narration on the exploits of buying the best pieces in the market—from choosing it right, to supervising the chopping and then finally, negotiating a price that is digestible.

If it is Sunday lunch, then the grand finale has to be tomato or dates chutney with papor (papad/popadams) followed by misthi (sweets). Mishti can either be a rosogolla or even packaged misthi doi from the supermarket.

With a *darun khelam* (fabulous meal), we have a happy and satiated Bengali family on a Sunday afternoon.

With so much bhaat, dal, bhaja, mangsho, maach and mishti in your belly, the body is bound to slow down. The grand meal has a soporific effect, and you retire for a well-deserved ghoom (sleep).

SEVEN

Pujo Pujo Bhaab

When the monsoon starts withdrawing and the sky is clear with a gentle breeze wafting across, it seems as if nature is signalling the arrival of Ma Durga, the mother deity revered by Bengalis. There is a term we Bengalis use to define this feeling—*pujo pujo bhaab* (the imminent Durga Puja festival). I think this feeling is a constant for any Bengali because it begins on Vijaya Dashami,[1] when Goddess Durga's idols are immersed, after which the Bengali clock starts ticking immediately in anticipation for next year's pujo. The thrill and anticipation of pujo just around the corner reach its crescendo a month prior as every Bengali will

---

1 Among Hindus, Vijaya Dashami marks the tenth and final day of the victory of good over evil.

There's a spring in his step when a Bengali knows Durja Puja is round the corner

see, hear and feel *pujo pujo bhaab* in everything around them.

You sniff the air and get the pujo vibe. The sweet smell of incense sticks gladdens your heart as you know that soon you will soak in the same ambience at a pandal (a temporary structure created to house idols for worship) in all its resplendence. The WhatsApp group of Bengali friends, dormant for most part of the year, suddenly comes to life before the start of festivities. Plans for meetups, bhog (food served to devotees after the offering), pandal hopping and gorging on delicacies are discussed down to the minutest detail. There are also phone calls from local Bengali associations seeking contributions and sponsorships for the festival. Bengali colleagues in offices, who have their homes and families back in Kolkata or West Bengal, look forward to their week-long leave for pujo with excitement evident on their faces. Everything around exudes the *pujo pujo bhaab*.

For me, *pujo pujo bhaab* is a trip down memory lane—my childhood memories of Durga Puja near my locality in the 1980s and the time spent with Ma, Baba and Dada at the pandal. I grew up in Govandi, a suburb after Chembur, on the Harbour line, which now goes all the way to distant parts of Navi Mumbai (a satellite township envisaged in the 1970s and is now a self-contained city). Mumbaikars mark their suburbs by three main local railway lines that criss-cross the city and its outskirts—Central, Western and Harbour. There were two Durga Puja celebrations in the suburb of Chembur back then. Having moved out of the suburb more than a decade ago, I am not sure if the count today has increased. In the 1980s, we used to frequent the pandal that was walking distance from our house.

While schools in West Bengal shut for the festivities, this is not the case in Mumbai. So, to celebrate Durga Puja meant either finishing school for the day and then visiting the pandals or taking leave of absence citing fever, cough and cold. I think the teachers somehow never believed the excuse of being sick and were sporting enough to just take it at face value. They knew that a Bengali girl or boy in school is likely to take leave during Durga Puja. And if one of the teachers happened to be a Bengali, then pray that you do not bump into her in the evening at one of the pandals!

The three to four days of festivities meant no cooking at home, providing much needed relief to Ma. Lunch was had at the pandal, which was bhog, served to all devotees at the venue. The bhog consisted of khichuri (mix of rice and lentils), the delectable labra (a mishmash of various vegetables) to go with the khichuri, tomato or date chutney, payesh (a sweet dish made of rice and milk) and a rosogolla. Families, including mine, carried tiffin boxes or utensils to be filled up with bhog and consumed again at dinner at home. In the evening, the bhog was heated up and eaten quickly so one could get ready for a visit to the pandal and watch various cultural programmes. One met many friends and acquaintances, flocked to the food stall selling delicious egg or chicken rolls, cutlets and other snacks and then settled down to watch the main programme of the evening, the showstopper—a Bengali movie.

The chairs that were lined up to seat the devotees were neatly arranged in rows, facing a large white cloth. There was an aisle and, at the centre, on a table was mounted the projector, to beam the movie onto the white cloth. Lights around the screen were switched off and darkness descended as viewers settled into their respective seats. The smell that wafted in the air was a mix of dhuno (incense sticks) and the aroma of delicacies from the nearby food stall. Somewhere ahead, a cigarette was lit (yes, smoking in public was allowed then) and the smoke mingled with the other smells to form a haze overhead. Suddenly, the white cloth would come to life with a series of crosses and dash images and then the movie started. The entire pandal was engulfed in silence as the audience watched the movie and the only other sound, apart from the dialogues, was the whirring of ceiling fans overhead.

Often, I would settle down in the chair, but soon my eyes would become heavy as sleep beckoned. I rested my head on Ma's lap and slept. The movie would go on till the wee hours of the morning and when it ended, Baba would pick me up and with my head resting on his shoulder, we all walked back home. I slept unhindered as Baba kept a steady pace even while carrying me.

The memories of going to the pandal as a child with my parents and brother is *pujo pujo bhaab* for me. I visited the same pandal after a couple of decades and all the scenes from my childhood immediately flashed in front of me. Like Baba, I too have held my daughter and watched the cultural programmes as she slept in my arms. So, *pujo pujo bhaab* is about beautiful memories from the past that remain hidden in the deepest crevices of my mind. The three words are like a password that magically opens a portal, taking me back to a time, when a small and happy world existed within the larger world.

So, the next time you say *pujo pujo bhaab*, close your eyes and travel back in time. It will bring a smile on your face and definitely accentuate the positive vibe that Ma Durga brings with her.

EIGHT

Bhog Prasad at the Durga Pandal

Till date, I have not seen the splendour of Durga Puja in Kolkata or anywhere in West Bengal. From my friends and acquaintances, I have heard, and I have seen on television—the grandeur, lights and decorative themes of Durga pandals across Kolkata and other areas.

While Durga pandals in Mumbai and its satellite towns do not compare to the lavish theme-based pandals in Kolkata, but I would like to believe that Mumbai scores over Kolkata in one significant area—feeding people bhog prasad[1] in a systematic and orderly manner. I am happy to be proven wrong, in which case my only defence would be that I had no idea about the scale of the festival in West Bengal

---

1 Bhog are food offered to God before being consumed.

Bhog prasad (offering) being cooked at a Durga Puja pandal

including the distribution of bhog prasad. Today, at Durga Puja pandals in Mumbai and its outskirts, thousands of people eat bhog prasad every day for three days of the festivities—Saptami, Ashtami and Navami. The Durga Puja festival among Bengalis is usually a five-day affair, beginning with Panchami (the fifth day) and the progressing on to Shoshti (sixth day), Saptami (seventh day), Ashtami (eighth day) and Navami (ninth day), culminating in Vijaya Dashmi, the tenth and final day of Durga Puja. In some places, people queue up, take the food, sit on the chairs and eat. In others, they are seated and bhog is

A food stall with heavy footfalls at a Durga Puja pandal

served by volunteers. There is no money charged for the bhog prasad, as the cost of organizing a Durga Puja largely comes from donations and sponsorships. People eat in batches and the crowd patiently waits for its turn to partake the bhog prasad.

Talking about volunteers, the few times I have actively volunteered at a Durga Puja event is when I was in my teens. I was in class VIII when I first volunteered to be a part of the team that was formed to serve bhobhog at the pandal. This was at the local Durga Puja pandal that I frequented in my childhood. Back then, the first job for volunteers would be to arrange the chairs in rows. These rows would have two chairs—one for sitting and the other as a makeshift table to keep the plate. Youngsters were made to arrange the chairs and do other sundry items before the heavy artillery, meaning the men carrying steaming steel buckets of food, trooped in.

After the chairs were arranged in neat rows, with enough space between two rows for movement, we were tasked with distributing plates. Plates, then, were made of sal leaves. Sal leaves are still used today but they are now more modular and plate-like in appearance. Once the plates were laid on the makeshift tables, water was served in plastic glasses. Often, the water was used to clean the leaf plate before food was served on it. Then came salt and a slice of lemon. Once the youngsters finished serving the necessary ingredients before the main course, dhak players started playing the dhak (drums) and, the food offered to the goddess Durga was brought to be distributed among the devotees sitting patiently. The offering made to Ma Durga was the first morsel placed on the plate. This was followed by a loud cry, '*Bolo, bolo Durga*

Mai ki! followed by '*jai!*' (Glory to Goddess Durga) from the crowd. Thus began the bhog distribution. Volunteers lined up with steaming steel buckets of khichuri, labra (mix vegetables) and beguni (batter-fried aubergine), going from row to row. We youngsters took a back seat then, for this heavy-duty distribution of the main course was meant for the grown-ups. There was an efficient supply chain in place; if a person serving khichuri noticed that the guests needed a second helping of the labra, he would shout, '*Labra lagbe!*' (Need more vegetable dish here!). It was similarly relayed by another man until another steaming bucket of labra was readied and dispatched to the designated row.

With khichuri and labra came chutney, made of either tomatoes or dates or a mix of both, along with papor (papad). This combination was divine. The youngsters were again drafted back for service, to serve the chutney and papad.

After the main course, came the desserts. Payesh (sweetened rice made in milk) was a constant; it still is and along with it, sometimes a piece of rosogolla or gulab jamun was served.

As the first batch of guests finished their meal, there would be another batch of devotees waiting patiently in a queue. Those who finished eating picked up their respective plates, put them into the dustbin, washed their hands and moved out of the pandal. The next batch would then sit down, and the youngsters would start the cycle all over again, beginning with the sal leaf plates. I recollect doing this for at least four or five rounds before most devotees had eaten to their fill, and it was the turn of the volunteers to sit down and partake of the delicious bhog prasad.

Even as the crowds thinned out from the main theatre, there was action at another counter. This was the counter for people to take the bhog prasad home, to be had for dinner. There were tiffin carriers, of all sizes, filled with food to be taken home.

Running around as a volunteer, in hot and humid conditions, was tiring but the sheer enthusiasm and excitement of being a part of community service ensured one sailed through it all with a smile.

In the evening, one strolled into the main area and the chairs that seated hundreds for lunch were now neatly arranged in rows, for viewers flocking in to watch cultural programmes. In one corner, the make-shift kitchen was buzzing with action. Ingredients needed for the bhog prasad were coming in; rice being boiled in large cauldrons and vegetables being chopped. Preparations had already started, to feed devotees who would flock the next day. For three days—Saptami, Ashtami and Navami, the kitchen fire roared and cooks sweated it out to dish out delicious food.

As seasons changed and one grew out of the teens and jumped onto the treadmill to get a job and secure a career, volunteering for Durga Puja stopped. But having bhog prasad did not, even though sometimes it is not possible to go to the pandal on all the three days to eat bhog.

Only once, a few years back, did I volunteer to be a part of the pujo committee. It is a committee formed to organize the festivities around Durga Puja. Within a few days, I opted out because it entailed devoting time, usually in the evenings, after work, every day for a month that continued till the end of the festivities. Unfortunately, I just could not afford to give it so much time. But here, I must express my heartfelt admiration for fellow committee members, for their diligence and commitment to present themselves every day, take up the jobs given to them and execute them, all while managing their personal and professional lives. I tip my hat to them. Further, sitting amongst fellow Bengalis, I soon realized that my command over Bangla left a lot to be desired. With my constant switching over to English and sometimes to Hindi, during a heated conversation with committee members, I realized that I was breaking the flow and rhythm of the conversation happening in Bangla. The frowns and raised eyebrows were fairly evident, as the group around me did not take too kindly to my sudden change of language, in what was meant to be a discussion in pure Bangla. I quietly retreated and kept my thoughts to myself.

The formation of a group of people, who come together for a cause or objective, is never devoid of one-upmanship and politicking. It cuts across communities, politics, society and even families. Soon, I noticed there were camps within the camp, with each one trying to further his or her agenda. There were a few neutral members like me, but there was a constant attempt to woo the independents, by sub-groups. So instead of getting sucked into the vortex, I decide to pull out while there was still time.

Over the years, I have noticed that Durga Puja, in a particular location, starts with all Bengalis coming together to celebrate the festivities. Over time, differences crop up and then a splinter group breaks away from the main body to form their own Durga Puja committee to celebrate pujo, in another location. From that splinter group emerges yet another faction, who then branch out to celebrate the festivities separately.

Factionalism notwithstanding, I must say that there has never been a shortage of volunteers when it comes to celebrating pujo across every location in Mumbai and around.

A jhaal muri stall in Kolkata

A Bengali family on vacation

Types of Bengalis

A khaddo-rosik (foodie) Bengali

A Bengali experiencing a ga-mej-mej-korche feeling (slightly feverish with mild body pain)

NINE

Pujor Chhuti

As Durga Puja nears, Bengalis residing in towns and cities across India for a living start making plans to go home for pujo. Over the years, across the many organizations I have worked at, Bengali colleagues hailing from Kolkata, West Bengal, or any other state, apply for week-long leave during Durga Puja. '*Baari jaabo*' (will go home) is the common dialogue when asked about plans for Durga Puja. The excitement in their voices is palpable, as the countdown to go home and be with their families begins the day their leave application is punched into the system. 'The organization can make me work during Diwali, Christmas or the New Year, I do not mind, but going home during pujo is a must and it is non-negotiable', remarked one Bengali colleague.

I wondered to myself whether the colleague will resign in protest if leave was not granted. I did not voice my thoughts to avoid an unpleasant reaction or a vociferous *cholbe na, cholbe na* (not happening) from my colleague.

Mumbai is my janmabhoomi (place of birth); it is also my karmabhoomi (place of work) so far. So, I have never experienced the excitement that a Bengali feels in anticipation of pujo holidays. I am yet to visit Kolkata during Durga Puja. I hope to go to Kolkata to soak in the pujo feel and I hope it will happen soon.

Growing up, it was school that prevented us from going to Kolkata for pujo. Schools in Mumbai remain open, unlike schools in West Bengal, during Durga Puja. More often than not, school during pujo was about preparations for mid-term exams, so taking leave from school for a week was out of question. Today, the cycle repeats itself with our daughter's school.

For me, pujor chhuti (puja holiday) was a Diwali vacation in Kolkata during Kali Puja, celebrated with equal aplomb as Durga Puja. The thrill and excitement of travelling to Kolkata during Diwali vacations is similar to the emotions I see my Bengali colleagues go through for Durga Puja.

A family at the railway station

The childhood memory of the excitement is still vivid. The day before departure was rife with frenetic activity at home, with Ma and Baba doing the packing. Dada and I were sometimes summoned to do odd jobs, like getting clothes out of the cupboard, but largely, we were told to stay away. Our scheduled departure was early morning and that meant reaching the railway station the night before. This was the 1980s, and there were very limited options in terms of transport, to get to the Chattrapati Shivaji Terminus (CST), then known as Victoria Terminus (VT), early morning. So, we spent the night in the waiting room of the station. For children, a

An attendant serving meals to the passengers

night in the wating room was nothing short of an adventure. Upon arrival, Baba would unroll the holdall, an important, large bag used while travelling long distance. Nowadays, I do not see a holdall, but the bag, true to its name, could hold all items from pillows to bed sheets to blankets. The holdall was rolled into the shape of a cylinder and tied with belts. Imagine a gigantic human size cigar in a standing position, which is how the holdall would look. Out

Vignettes of a train journey

of the holdall emerged bed sheets and pillows for us to sleep on, in the waiting room. But sleep was not on the list of things to do. The excitement of soaking in the sights and sounds of a railway station won hands down versus the stern orders from parents to get some sleep. Somewhere below, from one of the platforms, a train blew its whistle.

Is it leaving the station? Or arriving? I wondered. The waiting room door opened, and another family walked in. Where are they going? Kolkata or some other destination? Questions weighed heavy on my mind, and gradually, the eyes shut a little, only to open when there was some noise in the vicinity. The hide and seek with sleep continued till it was time for us to pack up and head to the railway platform. A railway porter came to take our bags and we all trooped towards the waiting train. The platform was abuzz with travellers hastening to board their respective compartments, and board. There were stalls, some on wheels, moving up and down the platform. We reached our compartment, boarding it in darkness. The lights inside the compartment were switched-on only once the train was ready to depart. In the play of faint light from the platform, fellow passengers were busy scouting for their respective berths. A man shouted out to his family member, to quickly move their bags to their assigned seat. Somewhere, another passenger announced loudly that their berths were in the next compartment. There was quite a bit of commotion. Baba located our seats, and the bags were pushed under the lowest berth, with a chain lock to ensure safety of our belongings. We would all settle down and I would immediately take the window seat. The reservation chart was pasted near the door of the compartment and Baba would deboard to take a quick look to check if our names were listed or not. This was a type of two-factor authentication to verify that we were indeed in the right compartment. The first factor being the name plate on the outer side of the compartment that said 'second class'. Sometimes, the plate was missing, and a railway official would come and write the classification in white chalk. The second factor was the reservation chart pasted near the door of the compartment.

At the scheduled time, the whistle blew and the train, with a push, left the station. Slowly, we left the station and the Mumbai skyline, as dawn broke, whizzed past. The holdall bag was unrolled to bring out the pillows and bed sheets out and I was told to sleep. But it was time to fight sleep again, for the wonders of the sights buzzing past the speeding train needed my undivided attention. However, this time around, sleep won as the steady rhythm of the train was soporific. I happily got onto the middle berth for some well-earned sleep, as the train sped towards Kolkata, where more excitement of meeting cousins and relatives awaited us. The wonder years are long gone, but the memories remain stored in one of the many compartments inside the brain. Writing this chapter brought memories connected to pujor chhuti, to the fore. One such memory etched in my mind is when we were coming back to Mumbai, after our holidays in Kolkata. As we alighted the train at CST, Ma remarked, 'The heart always feels light and is filled with joy when we are seated in the train going towards Kolkata. And it is heavy when we return to Mumbai.'

Yes Ma, the heart always feels light when I replay these precious memories, and it feels heavy when one alights from this train of thoughts and walks back into the present.

TEN

Wanderlust

Bengalis have a penchant for travel and the hills definitely figure among our most favourite destinations. So does the seaside! Almost all my relatives based in Kolkata and other parts of West Bengal have visited the temple town of Puri in Odisha. And they love it just as they gush over hill stations such as Darjeeling, Kalimpong and Gangtok, to name a few. I have, so far, not had the opportunity to visit Puri but have been to quite a few hill stations in the East and Northeast. I guess, the love for forests and hills, romanticized in books and movies by renowned Bengali authors and filmmakers, is part of every Bengali's DNA. It holds true for a probashi Bengali like me as well.

A Bengali family holidaying in the hills is a sight. Baba, Ma, poltu (son), dadu (grandfather),

A Bengali family on vacation

thammi (paternal grandmother) or didun (maternal grandmother) are all neatly wrapped up to brave the chill. There is a sweater, a muffler, a shawl and mankey tupi (monkey cap) to prevent the chill from entering the body and sending ripples down the spine. '*Uff ki thanda!*' (It's very cold) Baba remarks, despite the layers of woollens wrapped around his body. The mankey tupi is also a Bengali essential, particularly for children. '*Mankey tupi na porle, thanda lege jaabe*' (you will catch a cold if you do not wear the monkey cap), remarks Ma, as she puts the cap around poltu's head. Only poltu's eyes bristling with annoyance, are visible.

One interesting aspect I observed during my trips to Siliguri in north Bengal and Gangtok, the capital city of Sikkim, is the pice hotels serving reasonably priced Bengali food. I believe there are some pice hotels that are over a hundred years old that still exist in Kolkata too. The name comes from the lowest denomination of the Indian rupee; and in the early 1900s, these hotels catered to students and workers, serving them wholesome meals that were easy on the pocket. The pice hotels I saw in Siliguri and Gangtok satiated the hunger pangs of Bengali tourists by serving them *ghorer ranna* (homemade food).

Aajke ki ranna? (What is the menu today?) is the first question asked. Either a menu card is handed over, or the waiter will list out the items of the day. In one such restaurant (not a pice hotel) run by a Bengali; I observed how the owner displayed some smart marketing acumen to get the customer interested. 'Package *aache*,' (there is a package), the owner replied to the man asking questions on the menu on behalf of the group. The use of the word 'package' I thought was a smart one, for every product or service retailed today to customers is 'packaged'. In this case, the 'package' was a choice between a vegetarian and a non-vegetarian meal. 'Veg package *aache aar* non-veg package *aache*,' (there's vegetarian and non-vegetarian available), the owner announced. For a price of so and so, the vegetable package included gobindo bhog r bhaat with ghee (fragrant rice with ghee), moong or masur dal (lentils), bhaja (fritters), aloo posto (potatoes with poppy seeds) and dhokaar dalna (chickpeas patties, in a Bengali style gravy) with an assortment of desserts. The non-vegetarian package included rice, lentils, bhaja, aloo posto and then a choice between maach (fish), or dim (eggs) or mangsho (chicken). The potential customers then confabulated amongst themselves to decide who will eat what. Then, the man leading the group gave the vegetarian and non-vegetarian package orders to the waiter.

Talking about Bengali tourist groups, I noticed quite a few of them during my travels to Darjeeling and Gangtok. The group usually consists of a few families staying in a para (neighbourhood), who team up to form a touring party and go on a holiday together. Sure, there are economies of scale when one travels with a large group, but with different personalities, attitudes and habits coming together, it does lead to a few road bumps on the journey.

I once overheard an interesting exchange between a couple with children, who were part of one such group of Bengali tourists, from Kolkata. It was not exactly eavesdropping as the wife ensured she voiced her angst at a decibel level that would have echoed across the entire hill station. It was her lament on how nothing has changed for her, even when she is on vacation. She has to take care of the children here, just as she does back home in Kolkata.

'*Ek din o tumi dekhasona korle na*,' (Not even a day did you take care of) complained the Bengali lady loudly. In another location, a lady looking at her husband remarked loudly in Hindi, '*Tumne ek din bhi nahin sambhala bete ko. Joh sach hai woh hai*' (You have not bothered to take care of our son for even a day; that is the truth).

In both instances, the husbands' looked on impassively. One was courageous enough and wanted to retort in defence, but the wife did not allow him to continue. So, he lapsed into silence and walked ahead.

Differences also crop up within the touring party, over food. So, after a meal at a pre-determined restaurant, one will hear murmurs of disapproval. I wanted to eat fried rice, but Batul da (brother Batul) had already placed the food order, complained one man to his wife. Let us go out and eat separately in the evening, consoled the wife.

When it comes to members of a touring party, they can be classified in terms of their respective personalities. In the group, there will always be a sob-jaanta (mister know-it-all). It becomes evident to all, that he is the man in-charge—the alpha of the pack. And he does not take too kindly to any criticism or anyone questioning his authority or his planning. He is also an expert on the geography and topography of the destination—a walking, talking encyclopaedia.

The next is mister sob-jaanta's sidekick, who derives his heft in the group by siding and parroting what mister sob-jaanta says. He does not believe in expending energy unnecessarily by having a divergent viewpoint and is comfortable toeing the line that the alpha of the pack draws.

Various personalities in a Bengali tour party

In the touring party, there are a couple of people who are the work horses of the group. They do the heavy lifting—literally and figuratively—in the group. They do have a point of view, but they keep it to themselves.

The group is incomplete without one vociferous and argumentative member. He or she is always ready to give what he or she believes is a fitting riposte to every suggestion or point that mister sob-jaanta, his sidekick or anyone in the group, makes. After every such encounter, the argumentative member loudly swears his decision to never tour with them again. Come next year, the person joins forces and becomes part of the next outing. And the cycle continues.

ELEVEN

Aloo Bhaja

Among the food items that sit high on a Bengali's list, bhaja (deep fried fritters) is right on top. To me, bhaja is akin to a wingman in a Bengali plate full of food. It stands by you and supports you when needed. How? Say, the food on the plate is not to your liking and you grudgingly eat it; the bhaja arrives as a saviour and the sight of it gladdens your heart and you get the much-needed confidence to go through the entire meal.

Yes, bhaja evokes a very positive emotion among Bengalis. From potol (pointed gourd) to kumro (pumpkin) to begun (aubergine), we have a long list. But nothing, in my opinion, comes close to aloo bhaja (crispy potato fries).

Any comparison of our beloved aloo bhaja to continental French fries or potatoes wedges is

The distress in a Bengali household when there's no aloo bhaja (potato fritters) on the table

met with boiling rage; and the backlash is akin to sputtering hot oil in a vessel that can singe you badly.

There is always a voice in a Bengali family sitting for lunch or dinner, who will be the voice of all on the table asking the very pertinent question, '*Aajke aloo bhaja hoyeche?*' (Are there potato fritters today?). Any other bhaja, apart from aloo bhaja, is met with approval, but the heart beats with unprecedented

The different types of aloo bhaja (potato fritters)

enthusiasm if it is deep fried potatoes. Aloo bhaja wins the vote of the house with an overwhelming majority.

In a rare celestial occurrence where bhaja does not appear on the scene, there are always some murmurs of dissent and disappointment; before the eyes, hand and mouth go back to work in unison to devour what is on the plate, in absolute silence. If aloo bhaja is indeed part of the meal, there is a smile of approval all around.

Bengalis are definitely finicky about aloo bhaja. To some, it is jhuri (thin juliennes), to others pyaaj diye aloo bhaja (fried potatoes with onions) and to some, dumo aloo bhaja (cube shaped). My personal favourite is jhuri, and sometimes while frying, the potatoes stick together to become a single mass. One bite of this *muchmuche* (crispy) mass is a delight for me. I am sure that every Bengali household has its own unique way to prepare aloo bhaja.

Till date, I have not come across a Bengali who dislikes bhaja. There is always the possibility of reducing its consumption, owing to health and fitness reasons, but to completely give it up? '*Hobe na!*' (It will not happen).

Over the years, I have developed a habit of saving a bit of aloo bhaja on my plate, as a treat for the end of the meal. Chewing on muchmuche aloo bhaja at the end of the meal, for me, is divine. It is a habit I have passed onto our daughter, and I hope the baton of love for aloo bhaja is passed down to future generations too.

Aloo bhaja rocks!

TWELVE

Muchmuche

Be it a Bengali based in West Bengal or a probashi Bengali, bhaja has to be muchmuche.

To be honest, muchmuche never figured in my Bengali lexicon, and I did not even know its meaning. For me, a Mumbai-bred Bengali, the word muchmuche conjured up images of slippery and sloppy food. That is because in Mumbai one never had to use the Bengali term to define crispy deep fried food items.

I heard the word in conversations with Bengalis, but out of sheer embarrassment, never mustered the courage to ask them what it meant. Sure, I could have asked my parents, but for someone growing up in cosmopolitan Mumbai, where conversations at home were often sprinkled with a healthy mix

Bengalis' love for muchmuche (crispy)

of English, Hindi, sometimes even Marathi, it was perfectly acceptable to be culture agnostic.

Today, I can proudly say I know the meaning of the word muchmuche, an emotion attached with bhaja. Tele bhaja (puffed rice mixed in mustard oil and served with fritters) has to be muchmuche, for the crunch should travel from the mouth and hit the soul. Even the non-vegetarian bhaja, like a fish fry or

A muchmuche (crispy) conversation

a mutton cutlet, needs to be high on the muchmuche quotient.

For Bengalis, when it comes to fried fritters, 'crispy' has to be a crackle that reverberates. The positive reverberations then make a Bengali say the words that emanate from the soul, '*Bah, khub muchmuche hoiche!*' (Wow, It is very crispy!). Happiness and contentment radiate from the face and the eyes.

The crackle of aloo bhaja reminds me of an anecdote, from a few years back, when we went to

Kolkata to attend a marriage in the family. The caterer had arranged for a cook to deep fry the bhaja (fritters) at the venue. This was done to ensure that deep-fried items moved directly from the frying pan to the plate, thereby retaining their crispiness. A relative overseeing the frying remarked, 'Ek dom muchmuche hobe kintu' (it better be crispy). The cook, a veteran, who looked as if he could write a thesis on what it takes to make it muchmuche, paused, sized up the man, mentally scoffing at his naiveté, and gave what I thought was a brilliant riposte. '*Dada, amon cripsy hobe, pooro para sunte parbe*' (Sir, the crackle will reverberate across the neighbourhood). I noticed that he did not use the Bengali word, but threw in the English term, irrespective of the fact that he got the pronunciation wrong. But that is not important. The moot point being that the cook, with years of experience tucked under his gaamcha (towel) worn around his waist, very well knows the palate of his clientele, when it comes to deep fried food items. He does not need a johnny-come-lately to teach him the fine art of muchmuche.

Here is to the *cripsiness*, sorry, crispiness that defines our love for deep fried food. A crackling love affair with deep fried food—if one adds the letter 's', it certainly is 'smoochsmooche'!

THIRTEEN

Bhaat

This chapter is an ode to bhaat (rice). Every Bengali must have surely heard this line at least once in their life, while talking to a non-Bengali, 'you guys love maach-bhaat (fish curry and rice)'. While I am not fond of fish, my affinity and love for rice is as intense as any Bengali's across the globe.

I believe bhaat is at the centre of the Bengali gastronomical universe. A dollop of ghee (clarified butter) on steaming hot rice, makes for a heavenly combination. Pour some shorshe tel (mustard oil) onto the rice and have it with a green chilli. For a Bengali, this combination beats any dish produced by a Michelin star restaurant. Add boiled vegetables like potatoes, beans, bitter gourd; mix them with rice and a little ghee or shorshe tel or butter, and you

Bhaat: everytime and all the time!

have a satiating meal. Boiled eggs with shorshe tel, green chillies and raw onions are soul food for me.

Bhatè bhaat (boiled rice with various other boiled accompaniments), also called sheddo bhaat, is a constant in Bengali households. One can rustle up a quick wholesome meal with rice at the centre. Throw in eggs, beans, potatoes, okra and eggplant, to name a few, and voila! you have a complete, lip-smacking meal. To add flavour and tang to the boiled vegetables,

Quick recipes with bhaat (rice)

there are many creative options. Mash the potatoes, add finely chopped onions, chillies, butter, mustard oil or ghee and mix together. Have it with steaming rice. Pickles and papad also add to the zing.

You see, across all these preparations, rice is the common factor. For me, I may be having the most sumptuous of dishes, but without a little bit of rice, the meal seems incomplete. A small portion of dal and rice (lentils and rice), at the end, is enough to satiate my hunger.

Also, as a probashi Bengali born and brought up in Mumbai, I have had some delicious Marathi rice preparations like varan bhaat (steaming rice topped with clarified butter, ghee and lentil dal) and phodnicha bhaat (spicy rice tempered with spices) or north Indian rice preparations like rajma-chawal (rice with kidney beans curry) and kadhi-chawal (rice with yogurt curry) I am sure there are innumerable rice preparations across India.

To the culinary brains that have created these wonderful recipes, I must say, "Bhaat an idea, Sir ji!".

FOURTEEN

Boroline

This is a small chapter on a heritage brand that is a part of every Bengali household—Boroline (antiseptic, perfumed cream).

Even today, I remember the jingle 'khushboodar antiseptic cream Boroline' playing on the radio; it is a sweet walk down memory lane. The advertisement jingle and the distinct smell of Boroline evoke pure nostalgia. Boroline was a one-stop shop for any injury in the house. It seemed to have magical properties to cure every ailment—from dry skin to chapped lips.

It was an essential part of the Bengali family travel bag or holdall. I distinctly recollect a mother admonishing her child aloud for not applying Boroline, inside the train compartment. For that

Bengalis' love for Boroline

matter, growing up, 'Boroline *mekhe ja*', (apply Boroline) before stepping out to play with friends in the evening, was a common call from Ma to ensure protection from mosquito bites. Not sure if it helped but there was no way one could have stepped out to play without applying Boroline.

Long before Make-in-India happened, this brand epitomized the swadeshi cock-a-snook fervour to colonial rulers.

We Bengalis love Boroline as much as we love *lal oshudh* (a red liquid to apply on cuts and wounds). Lal oshudh was a must, like Boroline, in every Bengali household. I never liked lal oshudh as its colour resembled blood. I am not sure if it still exists, but Boroline stands strong even today. So, meme us, laugh at us for our ardent devotion to Boroline, *kintu* (but)!, if you ever tell us to stop using Boroline, then *shabdhaan*! *Bhishon gondogol ho jayega*! (Beware! There will be trouble).

So, what is your Boroline memory?

FIFTEEN

Satyajit Ray

My interest in the renowned filmmaker and auteur Satyajit Ray is recent, maybe spanning the past few years. But what was earlier just skimming the surface is now a deep dive into the vast and impressive body of work of this great man. Today, I read about him, watch his movies and as a cartoonist, go back to his drawings and sketches again and again, to try and absorb the nuances and subtleties of his drawings.

I am not good at drawing faces or doing caricatures; and it takes a lot of effort to draw a caricature of a well-known personality. But the work of this great man has become my muse. In the last few years, Satyajit Ray and his sketches and movies have been a rich vein of references for my sketches.

A pen sketch of Satyajit Ray

Although, I have not watched all the movies by Ray, there are a few, I consider personal favourites, that I have tuned into multiple times. Somehow, the stories and the characters in these films are etched in my memory, so much so, that I go back to watching them again and again. In this list are *Nayak* (actor) and *Chiriakhana* (the zoo), both starring the noted Bengali actor Uttam Kumar, who still stands tall among the pantheon of Bengali superstars.

Satyajit Ray with characters from his movies

In my opinion, in both the movies, Ray was able to peel off the stardom of Uttam Kumar and present him as an actor to the audience. In *Nayak*, in which he plays the role of a famous actor (almost himself), the conflict between the man and the star is beautifully captured. In *Chiriakhana* (the zoo),

A pencil sketch of Uttam Kumar from the movie
Chiriakhana *(Menagerie)*

Uttam Kumar plays detective Byomkesh Bakshi, whose intellectual prowess is wrapped inside a common looking man, devoid of any flamboyance. I feel that in both the movies, Uttam Kumar was in top-notch form and the credit is due to the man who could extract a performance that still connects with the audience—Satyajit Ray.

A pencil sketch of a scene from the movie Jana Aranya *(The Middleman).*

Another of Ray's movies that has a magnetic effect on me, is *Jana Aranya* (the middleman). This Bengali movie is based on a book, *Jana Aranya*, written by renowned writer Mani Shankar Mukherjee.

Every time I watch *Jana Aranya* or read the book, it unravels a new aspect of human personality and inter-personal relationships. It is like peeling an onion and every layer brings forth a dimension

A pen sketch of Satyajit Ray

hitherto unseen from when I watched it the last time. The movie is unabashed in its portrayal of the prevailing situation of the protagonist, Somnath, a young graduate in Kolkata. To me, every situation depicted in black and white in the movie, brings out the grey shades prevalent in our society, from unemployment to corruption, poverty to unethical practices.

Ray does not fool around in using the camera to project cynicism and the morass of depravation and degradation that exists in the society. Each character in *Jana Aranya* is memorable, particularly the great Utpal Dutt, who plays Bishuda, the mentor to the hero, teaching him the ropes of doing business.

His tone of condescension when the hero baulks at the idea of doing *baebsha* (business) hits a nerve. 'You can beg on the streets, but you will not get into business,' says Bishuda, taking a dig at societal dogma prevalent around starting a business back then.

Over the last few years, I have attempted to capture him and his work through my sketches. His vast body of work has been my muse for my drawings; be it through ball pen, pencil or charcoal pencil.

In the future, I will again watch his movies or read about him. And each time, I will pick up a pen or a pencil to sketch out what I have watched on screen or read. At a certain level, the work by Satyajit Ray is also fodder for my doodling and cartooning. What I feel for him and his seminal body of work is best captured in a line from his Bengali movie *Goopy Gyne, Bagha Byne*, which goes like: '*Maharaja, tomare salaam.*' (O great King, salute to you).

SIXTEEN

Durga Puja Chanda and Sponsorship

One term that is now almost non-existent during the Durga Puja festivities, in Mumbai, is chanda. Chanda is the money collected from families to organize Durga Puja. In the 1980s and even the early 1990s, a month or so before the festival, members of the pujo committee would do the rounds of various localities in and around the periphery of the event area, to collect chanda. The target audience for this collection were Bengali families. The collection drive would largely take place in the evenings. '*Pujo r chaanda nite eeschi*,' (We have come to collect money for Durga Puja) said one of the members standing at the door. I remember it was always a group of three to four people from the

Durga Puja committee members collecting chanda (donation) from a Bengali household

neighbourhood Durga Puja organizing committee. Most of them were known to Baba. After the usual pleasantries, one of the members pulled a receipt book out of a bag and asked, '*Koto likhbo?*' or '*Koto r kaatbo?*' (What shall we show on the receipt as your donation?). Baba would mention a figure. '*Ektu beshi hole bhalo hoi,*' (If you can please increase the amount) came a polite request as a response to the amount mentioned by Baba. If the amount was agreeable, Baba would give the money and a receipt along with an invitation card with details of the festivities would be promptly handed over.

The next few minutes were spent in general conversation and usually it would end with a question from one of the members, enquiring about which other houses in the locality could they visit to collect chanda. Their interest was piqued if they were told that there is a new Bengali family in the neighbourhood. Noting down the name and the address, the group would leave.

This was in the 1980s, and the monies collected from the chanda covered the costs of organizing the festivities. It was chanda along with a one-off generous donation from a patron that the organizing committee largely depended upon to conduct Durga Puja. From pandals to lighting to idols, priests, bhog prasad and cultural programmes, everything costs money. Until the early 1990s, chanda was the primary source to cover expenses. And I feel, with the liberalization of the country in the 1990s, Durga Puja festivities also opened up to the idea of sponsorships.

The days of committee members doing the rounds of Bengali homes are gone. So, instead of door to door, technology ensures the use of a jpeg image of the Durga Puja committee along with a pdf file of

A Durga Puja today replete with sponsorships

the rates for various sponsorships. This is widely shared over WhatsApp. Instead of '*chanda nite eeschi*' at the door, it is now '*ektu* sponsorship *dekho amarder jono*' (please try and get us sponsors) over a mobile phone call or a WhatsApp chat.

Back in the 1980s, the Durga pandal would largely be devoid of any banners or posters of brands. Today, every pandal will have banners or posters paid for by the brands. As the scale of some of the Durga

Pujas organized in Mumbai and adjoining areas has become bigger, so have the budgets. They now run into several lakh rupees and upwards. And the bulk of the costs are met through sponsorships.

They are of various kinds—sponsoring the daily puja rituals, garlands, fruits and flowers offered to the goddess and even bhog prasad. Brands take up space in the pandal area to set up stalls, and the popular ones with very heavy footfalls see a plethora—from real estate, banks, cosmetics, FMCG, food and beverages to automobiles—setting up stalls to do business or generate leads.

I remember, during the second year of the pandemic, when there were restrictions on assembly, the organizers ensured (for a fee) that the bhog prasad was delivered to homes on all three days. The plastic delivery containers were all branded with stickers of the Puja committee, a link to watch the rituals online and details to donate online.

Chanda as a form of revenue has today become almost non-existent. We now have sponsorships of various hue dotting the landscape in and around the Durga Puja pandal.

Epilogue

It threw a plume of dust when I reached for it. I brushed the coat of dust on a diary from 1961 that was lying in one corner of the cupboard. The pages thew up images and lot of memories. As I flipped the pages of the diary, I realized that the passion for cartooning comes from someone very close, my baba (father). And this diary played an important role in laying the foundation for my love for doodling, in my formative years.

The diary maintained by Baba has pen drawings and cartoons, sketched by him. It is a personal diary with essays, observations and even expense statements written by him. Most of the writing are in Bengali. His sketches ranged from political and social ones to even a sketch of a cricket field in the shape of a cricket bat, with the names of the field positions written in Bengali! That is very creative, I think. It was also a personal diary with day expense statements, the summary of a telegram sent with lines like 'Myself well, letter to follow', as his family anxiously waited for a letter from him. It even had events of the day jotted down, including the day he set foot in Mumbai (Bombay then) in 1963, with details like arrival by train, taxi fare and even cooking on a stove. The diary was a chronicle of his initial days as a bachelor in Mumbai. Like a true Bengali, he even expressed his immense happiness for the availability of a variety of maach.

As I flipped page after page, going back in time, I stopped at one sketch, over which there were outlines hurriedly drawn. These were my over lines on the drawing. I do not remember how old I was then, but I now know that my love for drawing were sowed in those over lines that I absent-mindedly scribbled back then. I guess it remained etched in my subconscious, lying dormant, as I got busy with building a career, a family and went after other material pursuits. Thankfully, it has emerged again in the past few years and has now become a serious habit. A habit I hope to make time for and continue no matter the ups and downs of life that await me ahead.

Possibly, Baba's passion for sketching followed the same trajectory. I never saw him sit down and sketch, as he was busy trying hard to give a comfortable life to his family. Only once did he pick up the paintbrush to paint a beautiful landscape in my school drawing book. It was an assignment I had missed, and Baba ensured that he finished the drawing overnight, so I could submit it on time the next day.

Before, the diary was one of the many things lying in the house. Today, it is precious and more valuable than any material possession I have. The diary with its drawings is like the heart that pumps my love for cartooning, which now flows in my veins. It had paused for some time but is now flowing seamlessly.

I lost Baba early in life, so there are a lot of unsaid things to ask and share, including his notes and drawings from the diary. What was he thinking when he put pen to paper; did he wish to write or draw? What does he think of my sketches? Perhaps, one day, on the other side, I will meet him and discuss the diary, its contents, his sketches and so many other things.

And amidst so many unfinished topics to converse about, I would like to just tell him, 'Thank you, Baba, for allowing me to draw the over lines on your sketches when I was a child.'

It was these lines that laid the foundation, and if you were around today, you would not overtly express but silently approve of my pursuit.

So, when it comes to cartooning, I guess you can say I am a chip off the old block!

About the Author

Rajiv Banerjee is a self-taught cartoonist, an ex-journalist and a successful corporate communications leader. Rajiv's love for cartooning began at the age of six, watching his father create witty cartoons in a little black diary. The primary source of inspiration and learning the craft, thereafter, has been the works of renowned cartoonists such as R.K. Laxman, Mario Miranda and Ajit Ninan.

On the professional front, Rajiv currently works as the head of corporate communications at a leading business conglomerate. Prior to that, he spent a decade at one of the largest private sector banks in a similar role. Before switching over to the corporate side, he was a journalist and served as the editor of Brand Equity, the advertising and marketing supplement of the *Economic Times*, where he worked for close to a decade, writing, editing and conceptualizing news and features stories. By then, he had dabbled in television and online media.

Rajiv holds a twin bachelor's degree in commerce and law and a certificate in Advanced Management in Public Policy from ISB, Hyderabad. He lives in Navi Mumbai with his wife, Indrani, their fourteen-year-old daughter, Rahini, and three-year-old Golden Retriever son, Cooper.

www.ingramcontent.com/pod-product-compliance
Lightning Source LLC
LaVergne TN
LVHW041531070526
838199LV00046B/1616